Based on an original idea by Alex A.

First published in French in 2014 by Presses Aventure under the title
L'ultime symbole absolu.

Adventure Press Inc.
55 Jean-Talon Street West
Montreal, Quebec, Canada H2R 2W8
adventurepress.ca

President and CEO: Marc G. Alain
Editor: Marie-Eve Labelle
Page layout: Vicky Masse
Translator: Rhonda Mullins
Proofreader: Sasha Regehr

Legal deposit – Bibliothèque et Archives nationales du Québec, 2017
Legal deposit – Library and Archives Canada, 2017

ISBN: 978-1-77285-014-7 (PAPERBACK)

ISBN: 978-1-77285-015-4 (PDF)
ISBN: 978-1-77285-016-1 (EPUB)
ISBN: 978-1-77285-017-8 (KINDLE)

Government of Quebec – Tax credit for book publishing and Business support
program for books and specialized publishing – SODEC

Funded by the government of Canada

Printed in China

THE ULTIMATE SYMBOL

WRITTEN AND ILLUSTRATED BY ALEX A.

ADVENTURE PRESS

FOR VANESSA, TO WHOM I OWE
THE FOX CHARACTER ON PAGE 6...
AND ALL MY FUTURE FOX CHARACTERS.

THE REDLANDS...

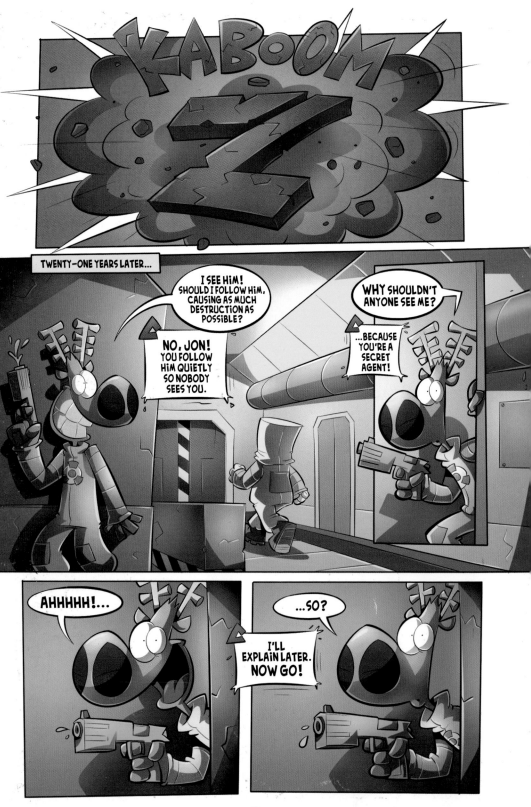

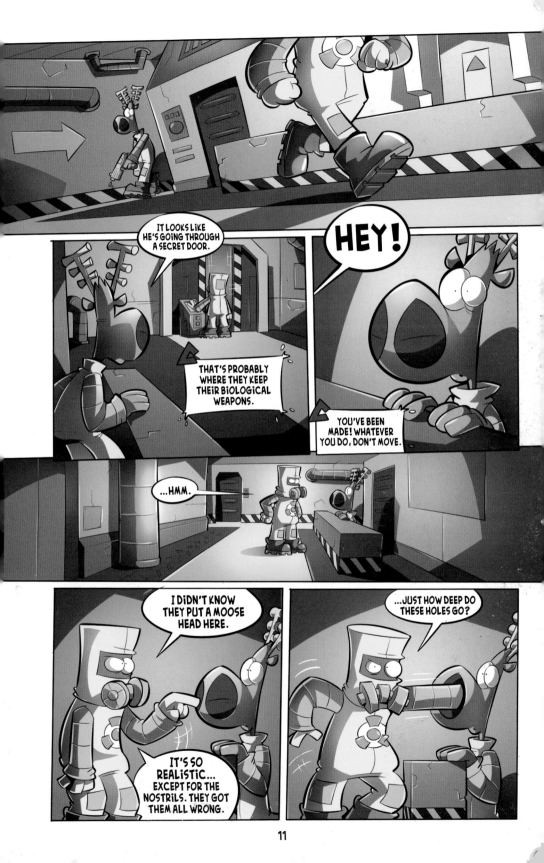

12

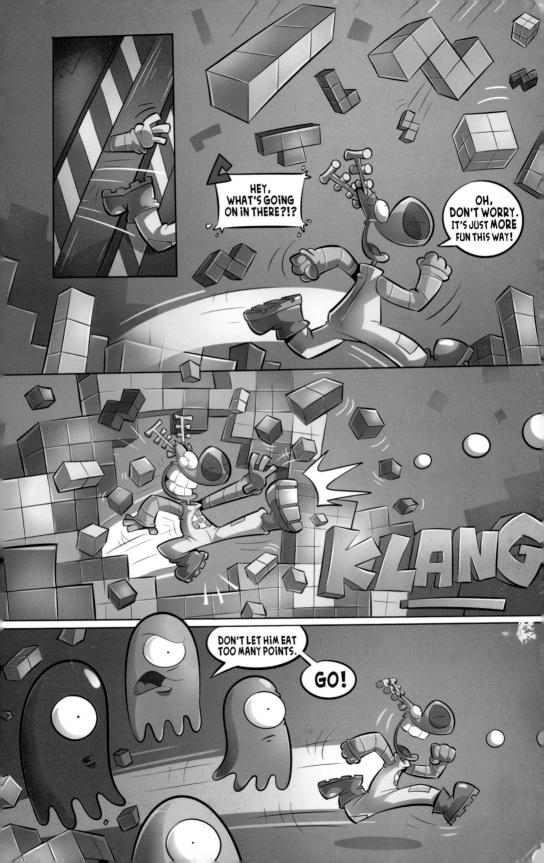

14

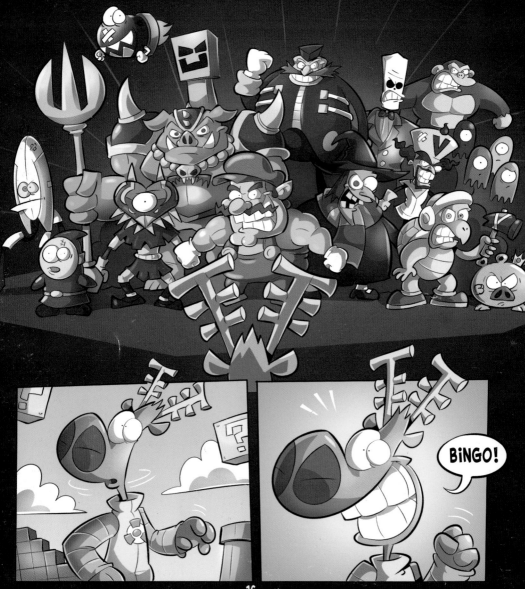

BiNGO!

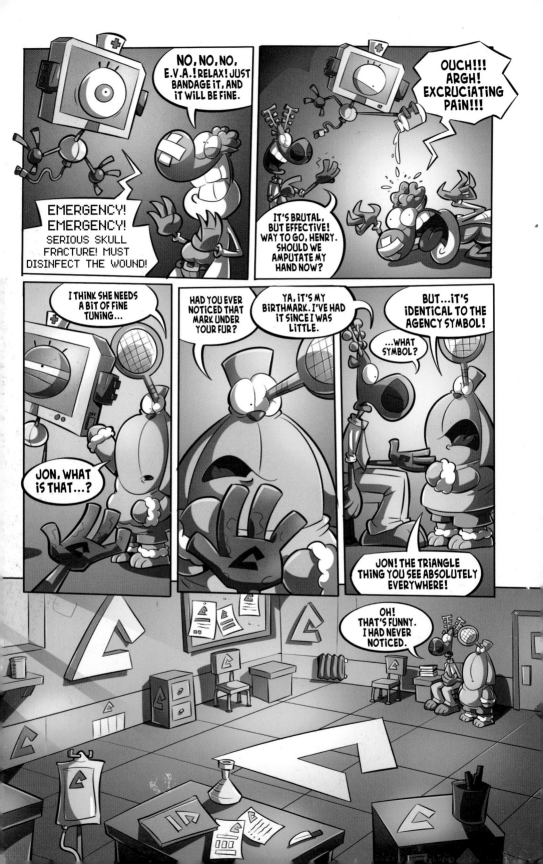

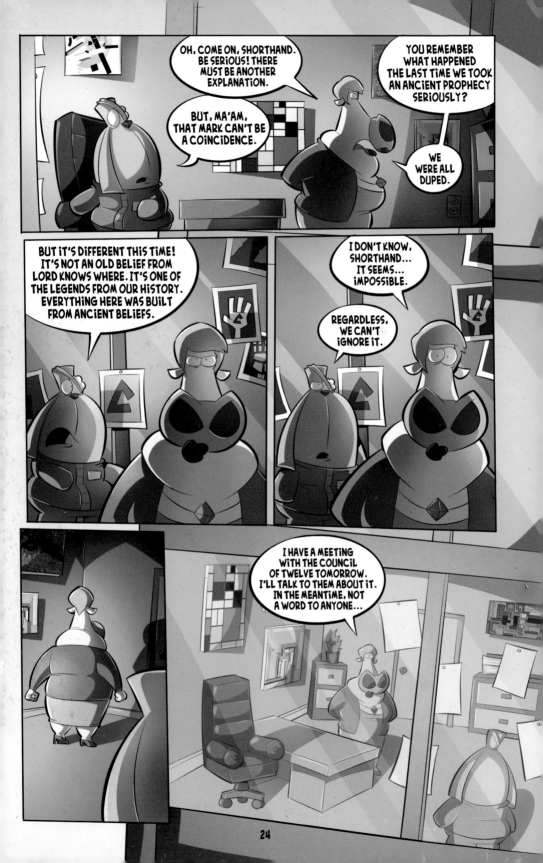

24

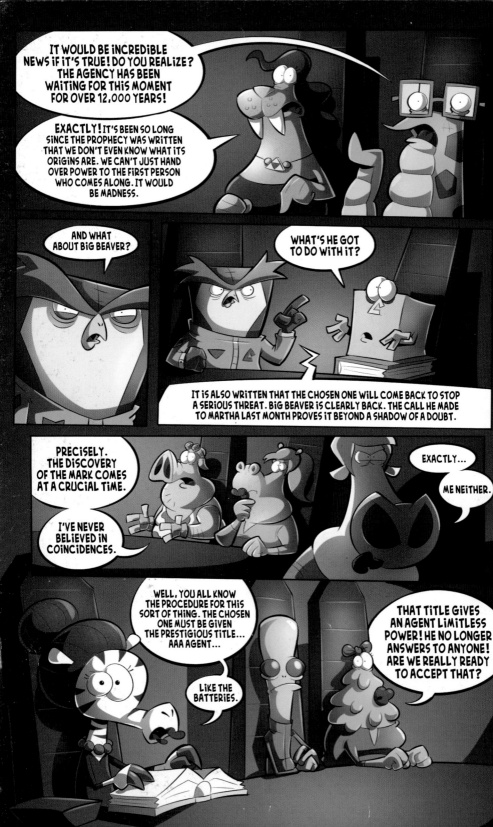

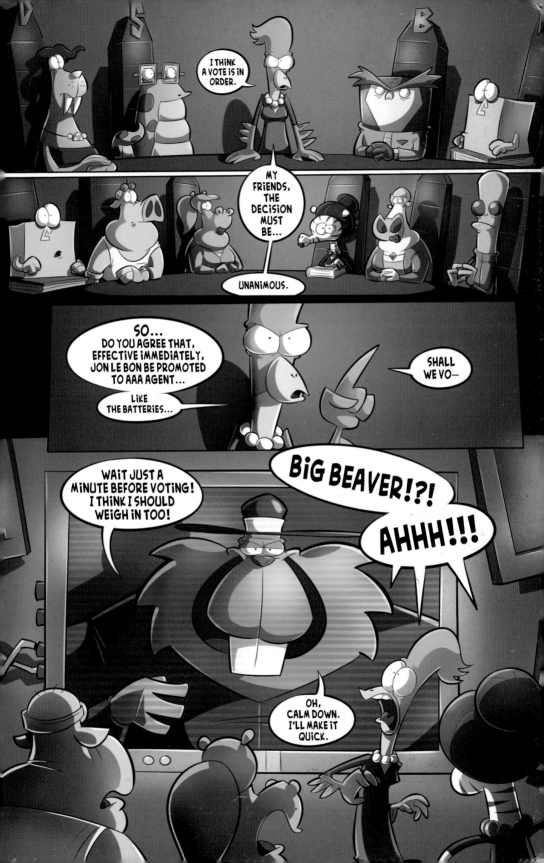

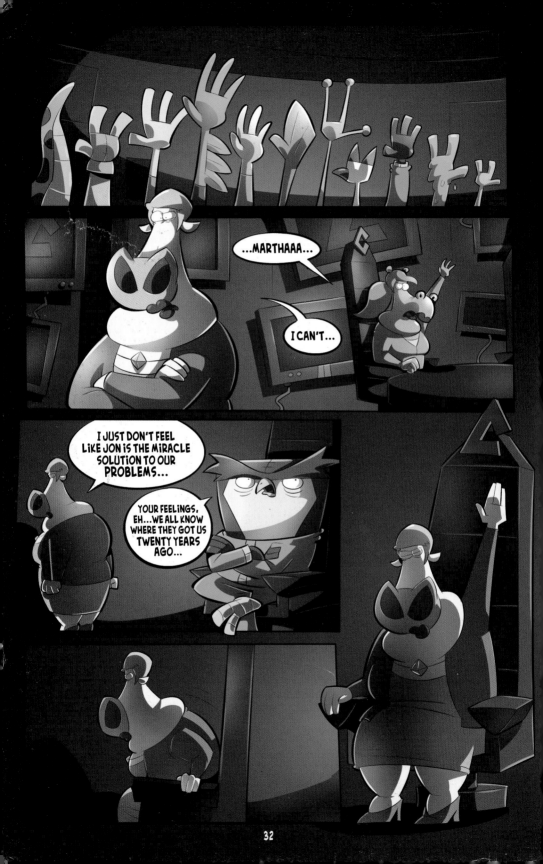

35

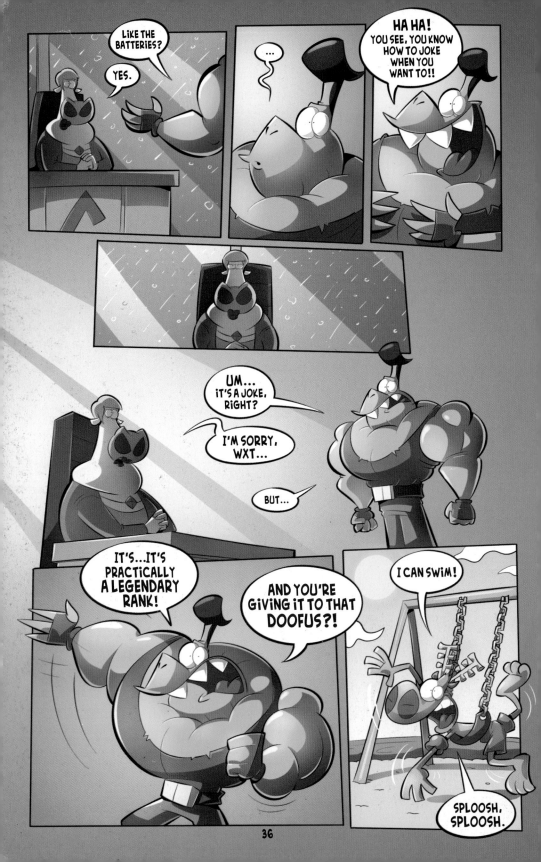

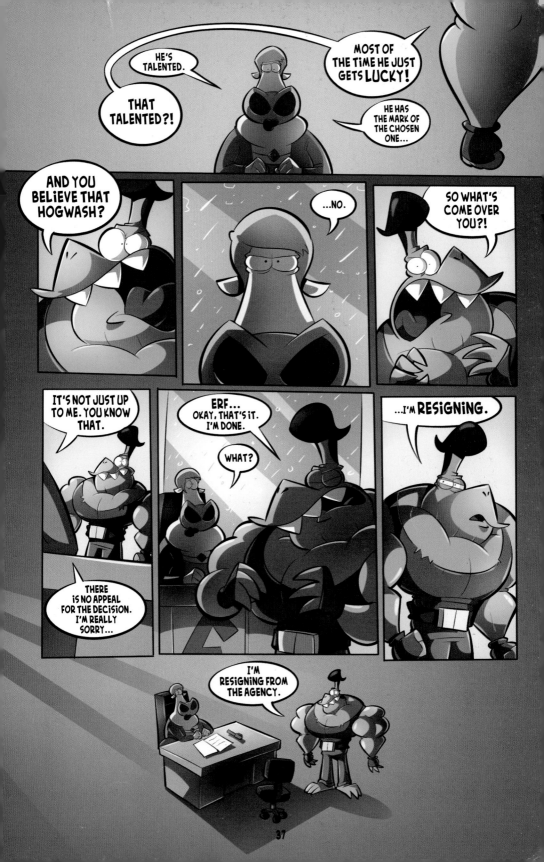

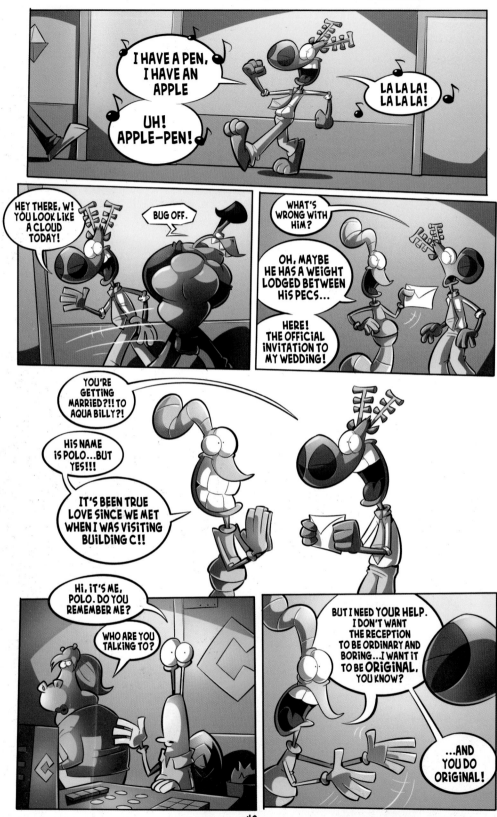

43

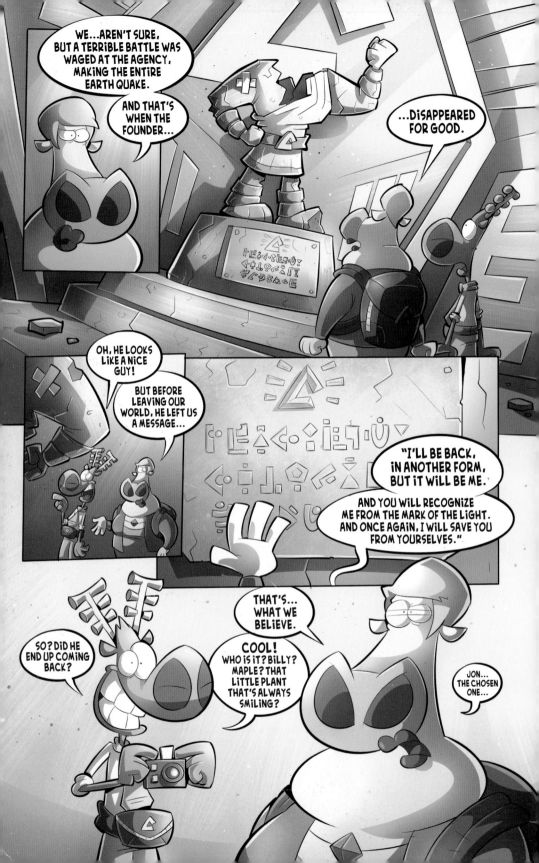

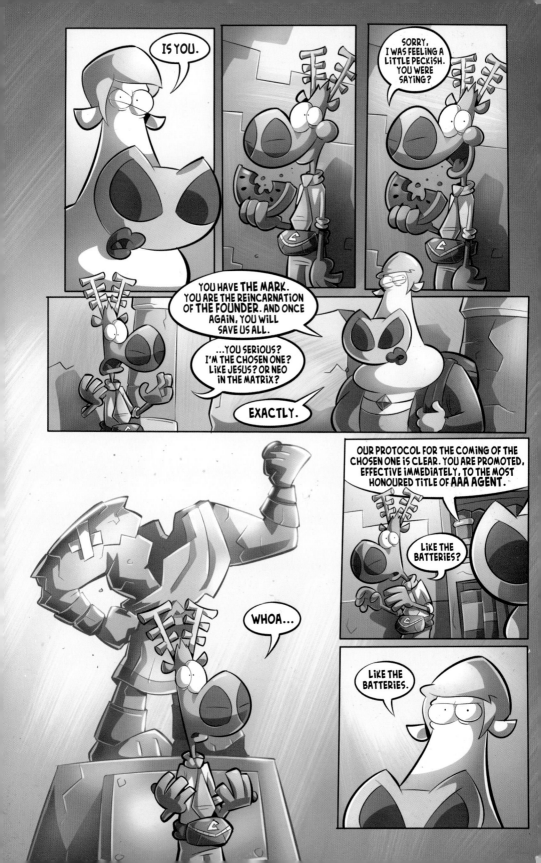

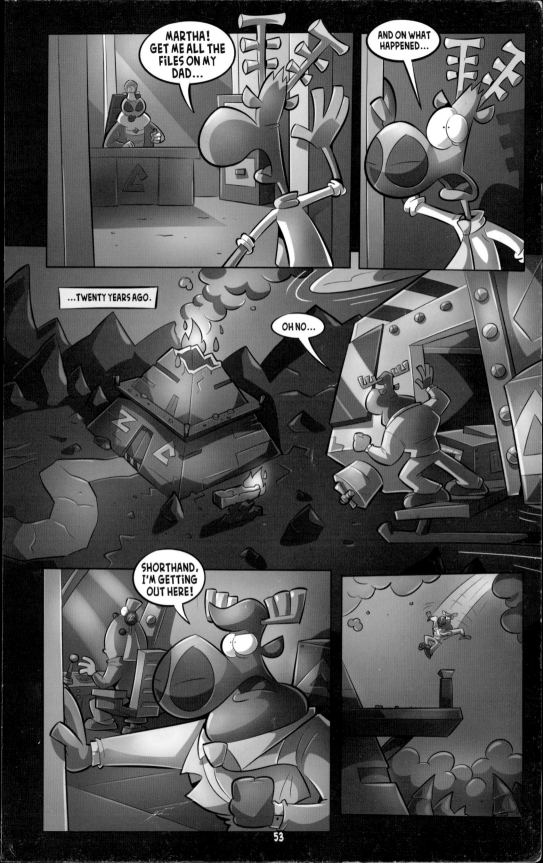

WOW! MY DAD WAS QUITE THE HERO!

HI! DOES THE CHOSEN ONE NEED ANY HELP?

HA HA! ALWAYS! COME ON IN.

WHAT ARE WE LOOKING FOR?

HOW BIG BEAVER HACKED INTO THE COMMUNICATION SYSTEM, AND WHAT HIS PLAN IS.

HMM...AND YOU'RE LOOKING FOR CLUES FROM HIS PAST BEHAVIOUR?

YEP! HE'S QUITE THE BAD GUY! I UNDERSTAND WHY EVERYONE AT THE AGENCY IS SO AFRAID OF HIM.

AND ARE YOU SCARED?

I THINK HE'S PRETTY COOL, ACTUALLY!

HMM...DIDN'T ANYONE EVER TELL YOU TO...

WATCH OUT FOR ARCH VILLAINS, I KNOW!

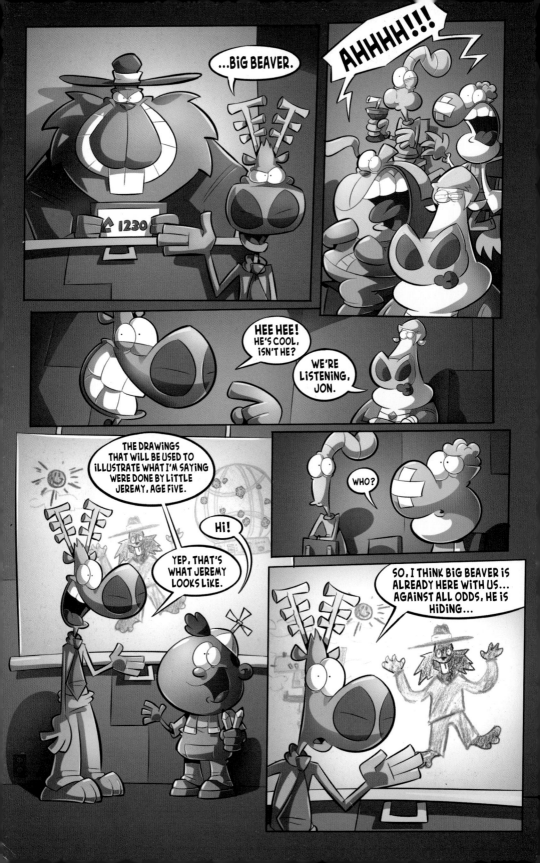

HERE. IN BUILDING T, CURRENTLY UNDER CONSTRUCTION IN THE PACIFIC OCEAN.

I NOTICED IN THE FILES THAT THE BUILDING IS POWERED WITH A GRAVITON RESERVOIR...

A BRAND-NEW FORM OF ENERGY THAT AGENCY SCIENTISTS HAVE ONLY JUST DISCOVERED.

WHAT MAKES YOU SAY THAT?

I WORKED ON IT!

SO IT WOULD BE THE IDEAL HIDING SPOT FOR BIG BEAVER. NEARBY, BUT INVISIBLE.

SINCE IT'S A VERY POWERFUL FORM OF ENERGY, AND STILL LITTLE UNDERSTOOD, IT TENDS TO SCRAMBLE EVEN OUR MOST POWERFUL DETECTORS.

FROM THERE HE HAS ACCESS TO ALL THE TECHNOLOGY IN THE BUILDING. HE HAS ALREADY STARTED TO HACK INTO OUR COMMUNICATIONS.

SO ANYONE NEAR THIS RESERVOIR WOULD BE UNDETECTABLE TO US.

HE'S JUST REPEATING WHAT HE TRIED TO DO TWENTY YEARS AGO.

BUT HE'LL GO FURTHER THIS TIME...

69

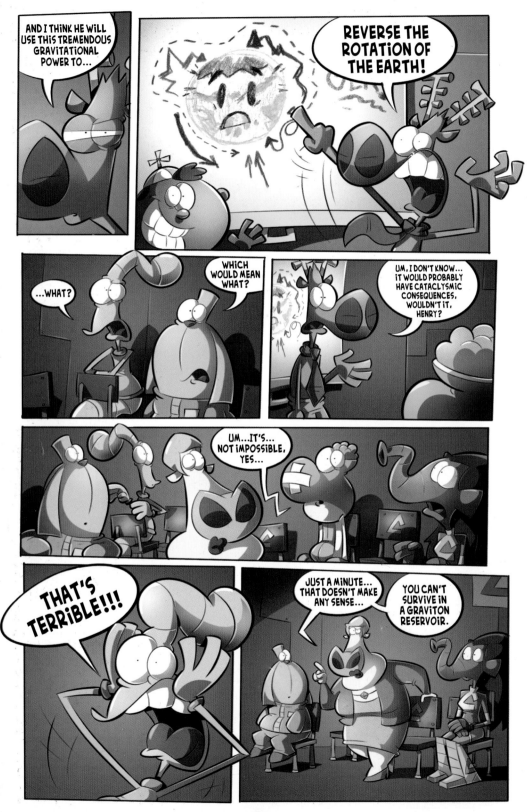

70

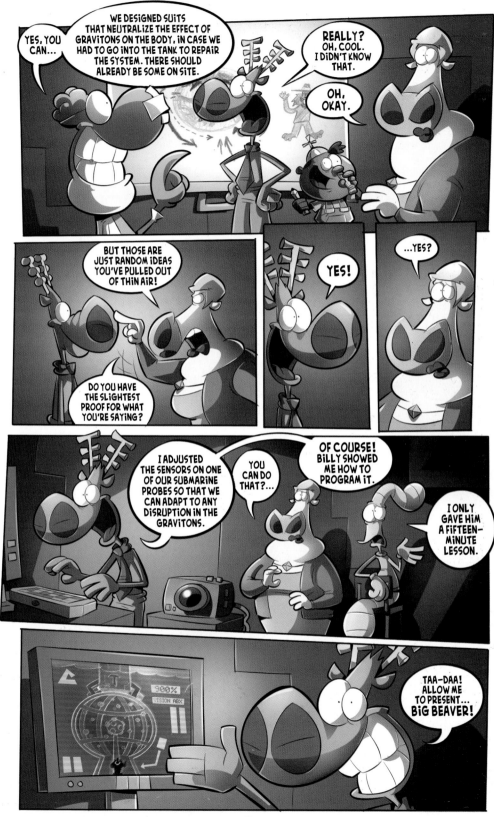

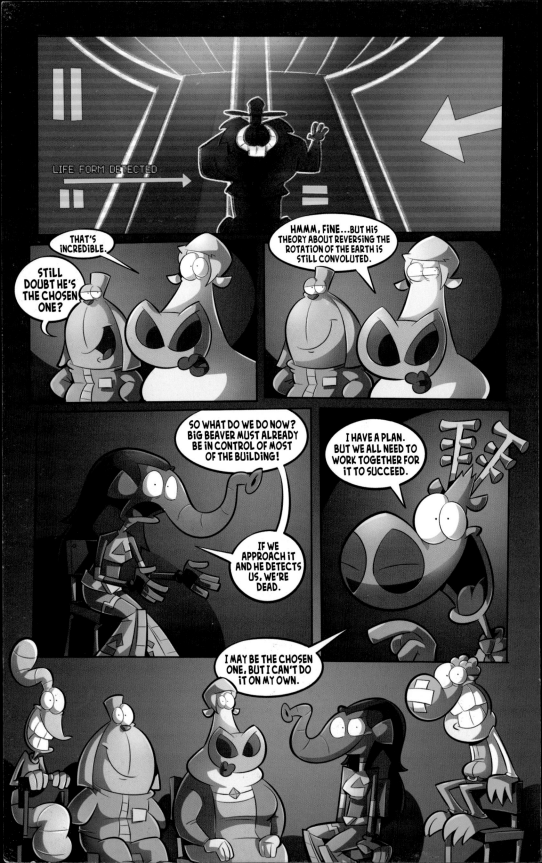

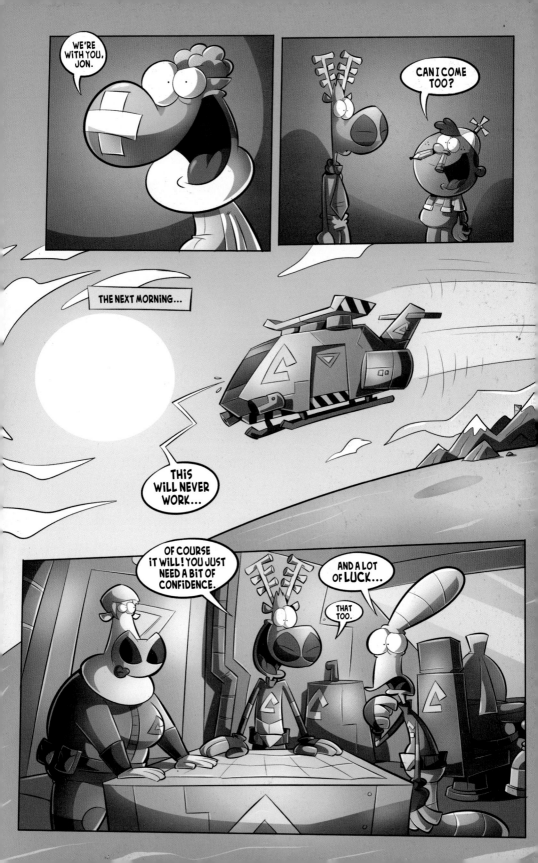

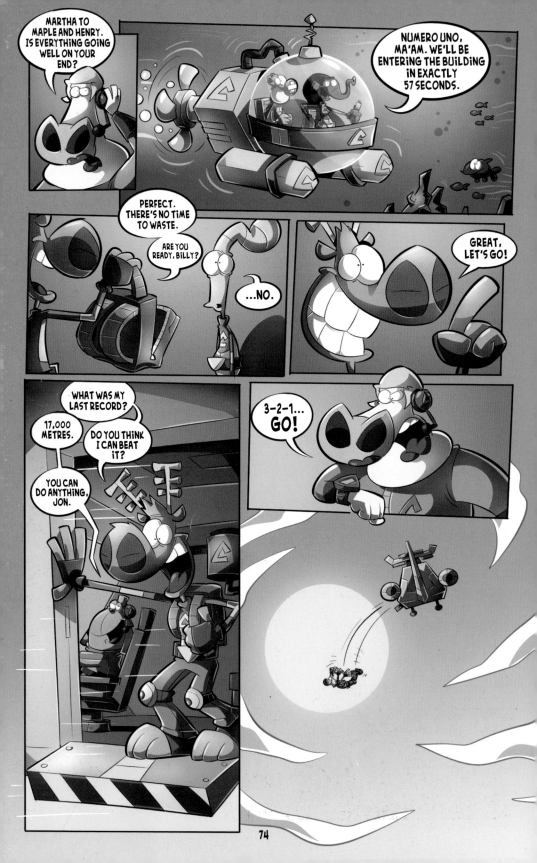

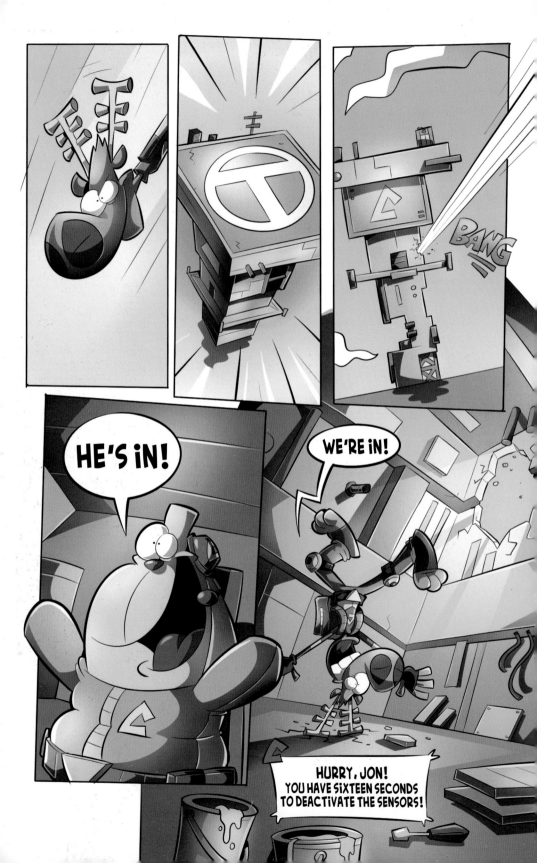

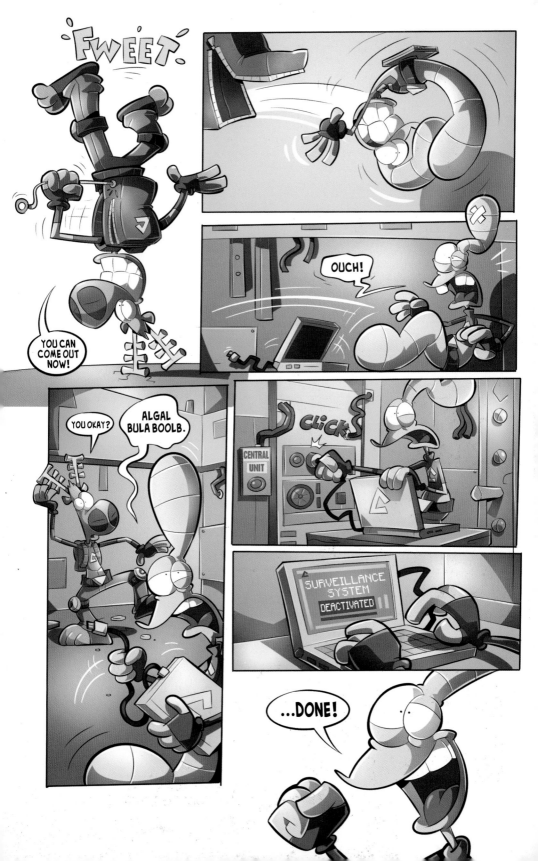

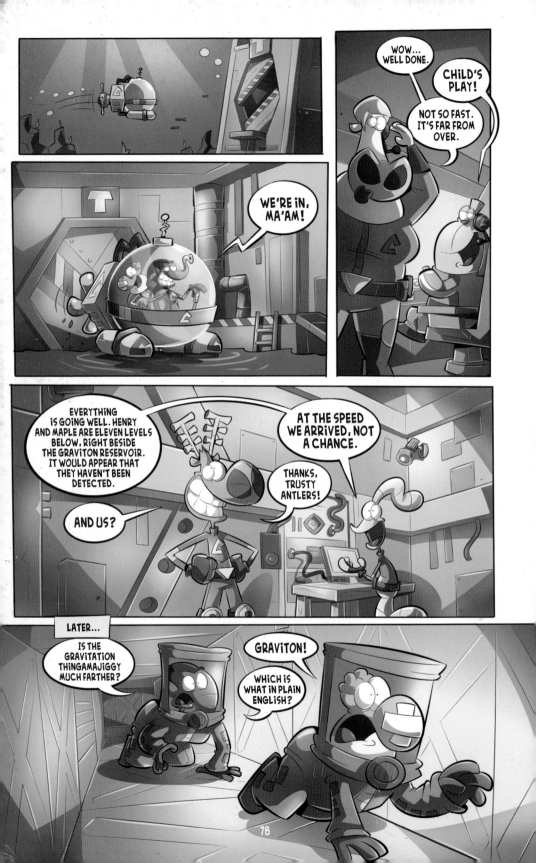

WOW... WELL DONE.

CHILD'S PLAY!

NOT SO FAST. IT'S FAR FROM OVER.

WE'RE IN, MA'AM!

EVERYTHING IS GOING WELL. HENRY AND MAPLE ARE ELEVEN LEVELS BELOW, RIGHT BESIDE THE GRAVITON RESERVOIR. IT WOULD APPEAR THAT THEY HAVEN'T BEEN DETECTED.

AND US?

AT THE SPEED WE ARRIVED, NOT A CHANCE.

THANKS, TRUSTY ANTLERS!

LATER...

IS THE GRAVITATION THINGAMAJIGGY MUCH FARTHER?

GRAVITON!

WHICH IS WHAT IN PLAIN ENGLISH?

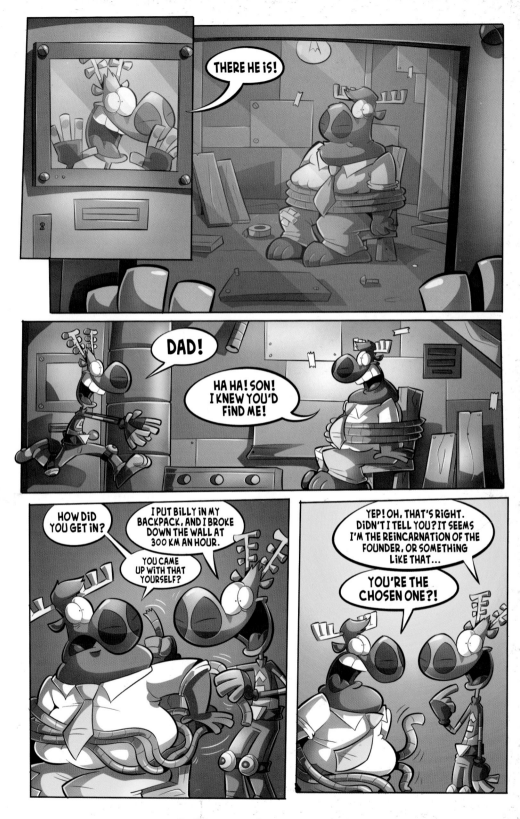

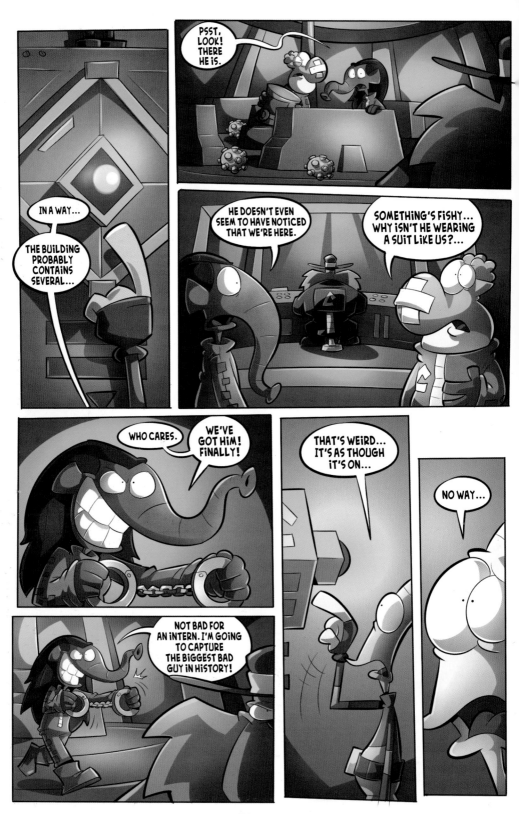

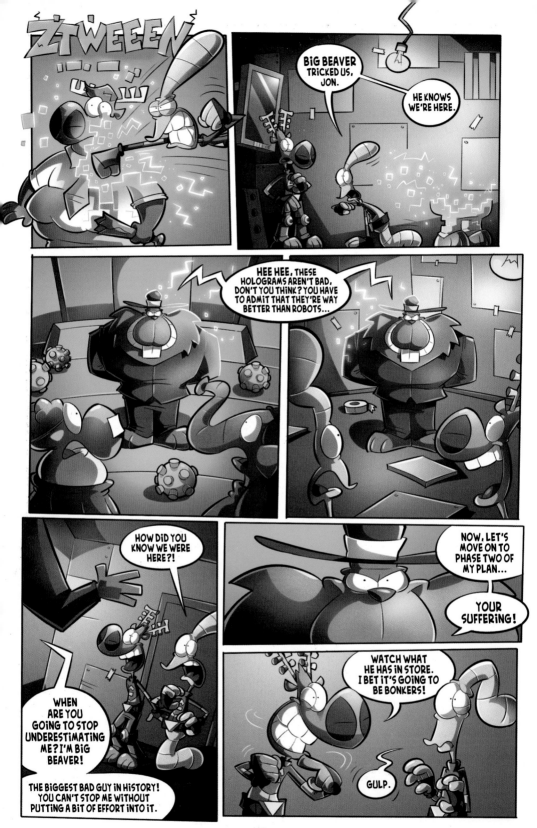

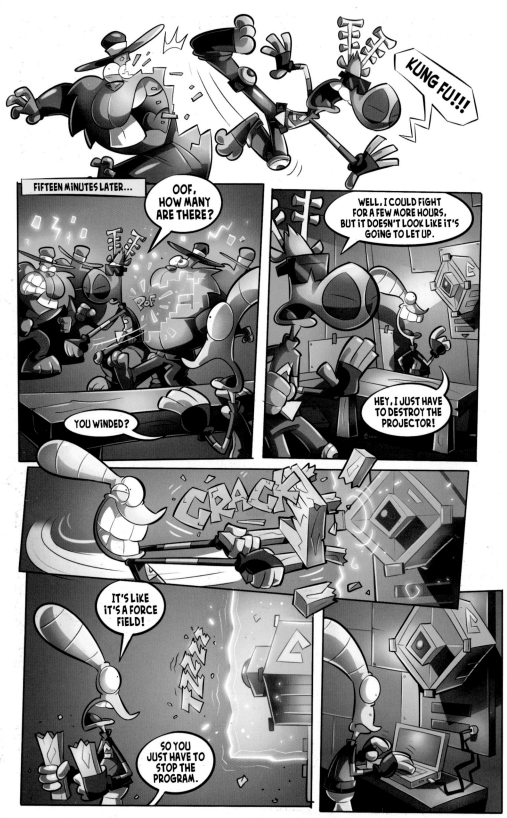

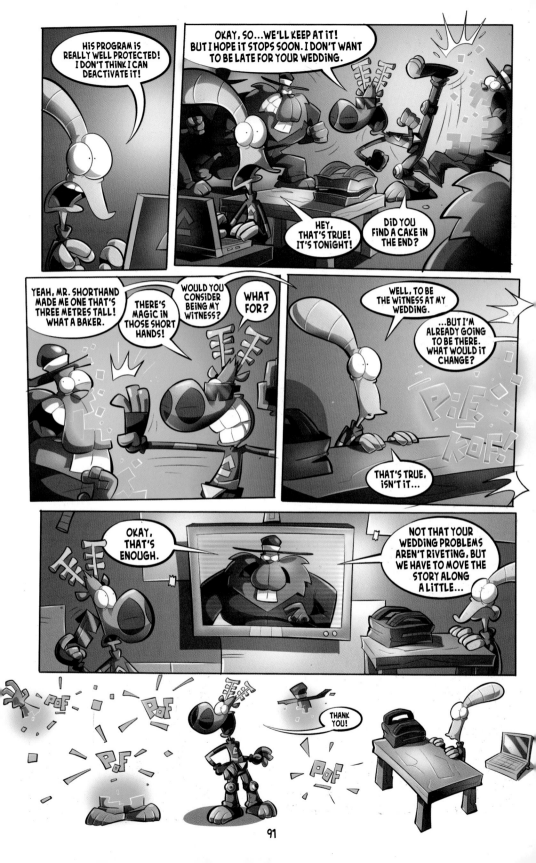

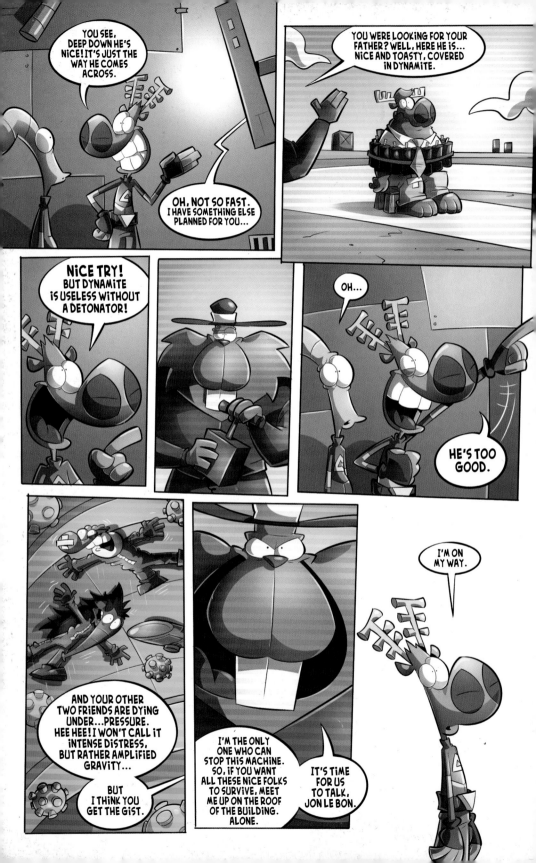

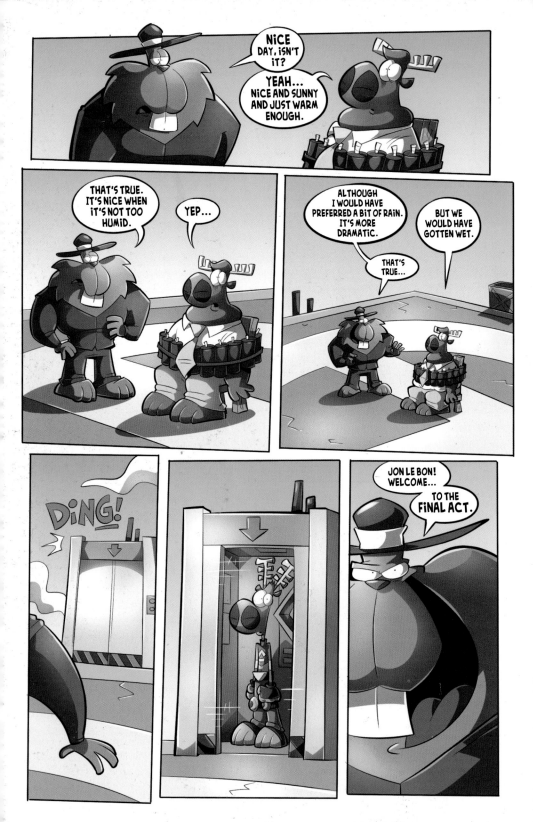

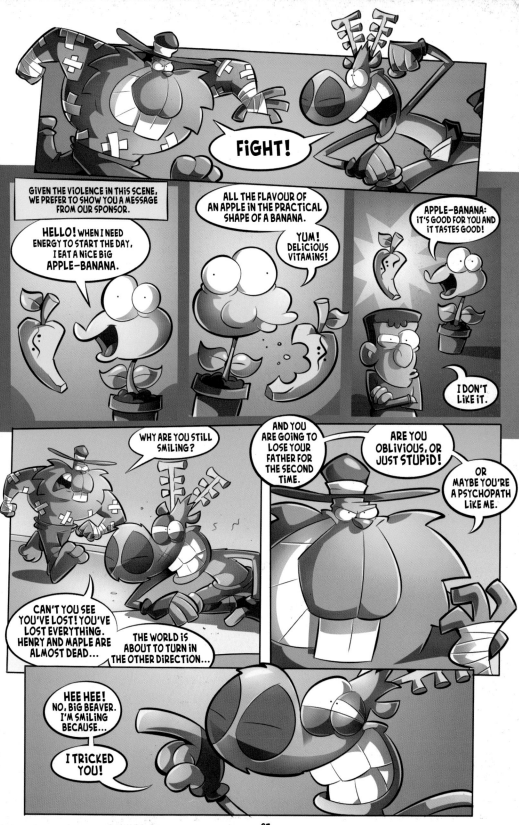

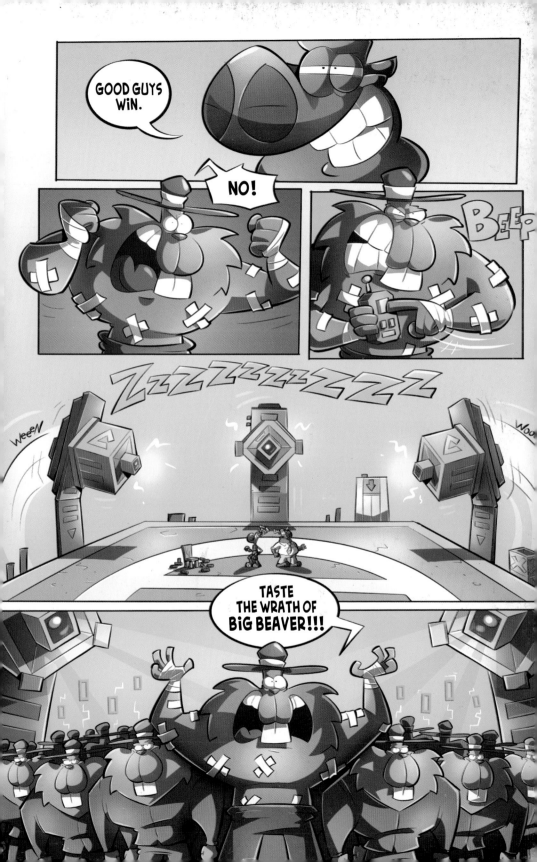

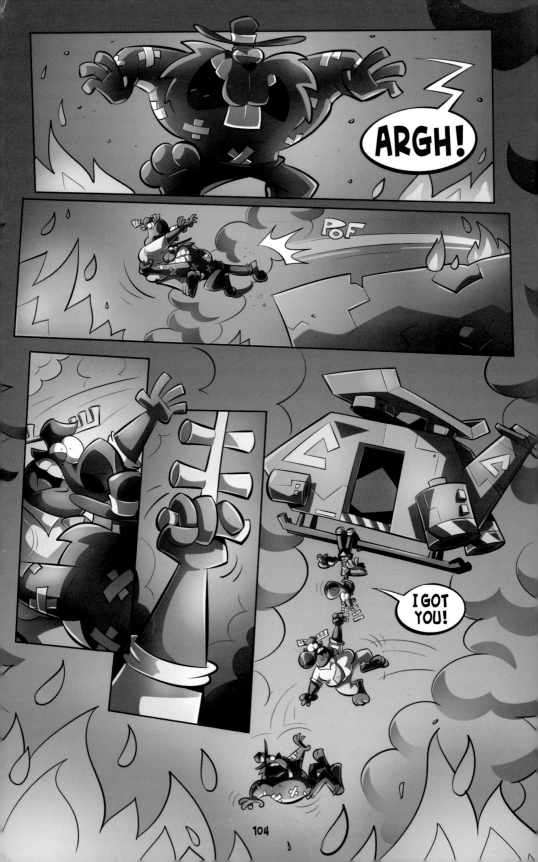

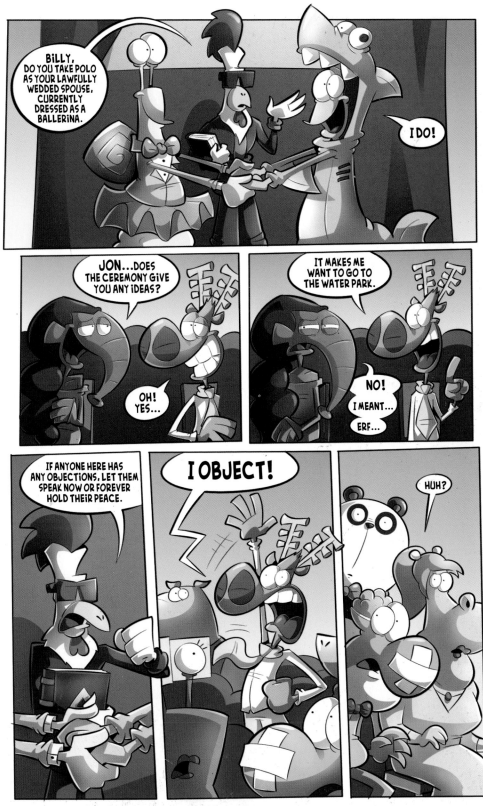

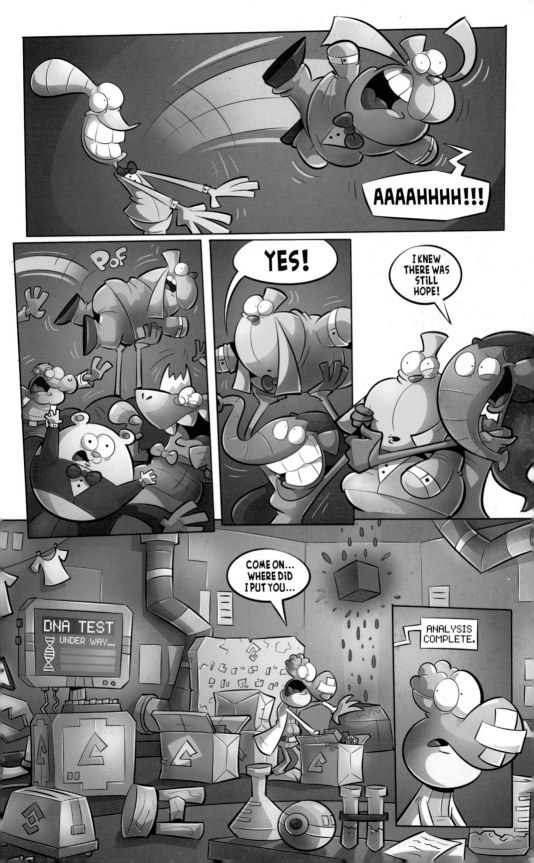

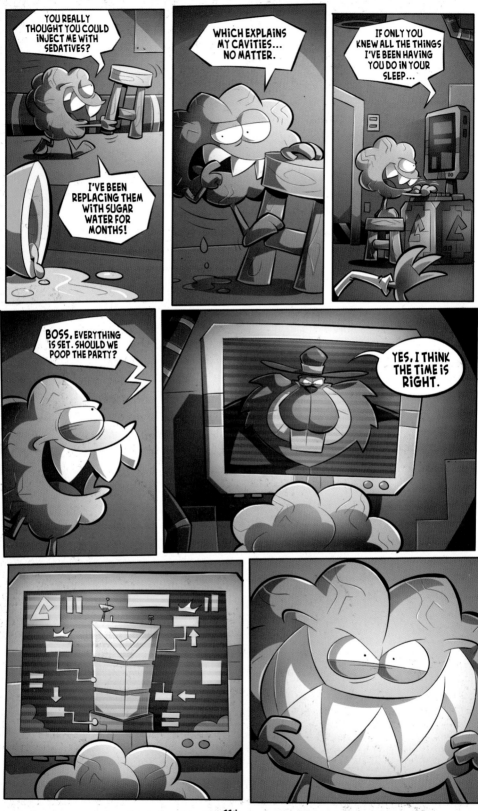

Alex A. is both author and illustrator of *Super Agent Jon Le Bon*. He discovered his love for drawing and creating cartoon characters at the early age of eight and has been at it ever since. His limitless imagination allows him to create new plots and twists and even completely new universes for his wacky and offbeat characters to evolve.

He'll tell you that his main source of inspiration is "all that exists but especially all that doesn't exist but lives in my imagination."

He's been successful as a freelance illustrator for books and magazines but his drive and determination has gotten him where he really wants to be — developing and drawing his own series.

The creation of *Super Agent Jon Le Bon* is the culmination of many years of work, and gives us a series that is both very unique, intriguing and totally hilarious. Jon Le Bon, because of his innocence and fearlessness, can get himself in all sorts of trouble — but there's nothing he can't handle with a little help from his friends.

 Alex A. lives in Montreal with his dog, Wolfy, and always shows up for book signings in his distinctive wool hat and colorful plaid pants, ready to entertain his young readers.

THE BRAIN OF THE APOCALYPSE

FORMULA V

A GRAPHIC NOVEL SERIES THAT'S FUNNY, OFFBEAT AND BRILLIANT!

OPERATION SHORTHAND

THE PROPHECY OF FOUR

TIME TRAVEL FRIDGE

A SHEEP IN THE HEAD

THE ULTIMATE SYMBOL

BEAVER FOREVER

COMING IN 2018

124